Life Goes On

Day-to-Day Stories and Language Activities

HIGH BEGINNING

Ann Gianola

Instructor, San Diego Community College District
Instructor, University of San Diego English Language Academy
San Diego, California

New Readers Press

Life Goes On: Day-to-Day Stories and Language Activities
High-Beginning Level
ISBN 978-1-56420-792-0

Copyright © 2009 New Readers Press
New Readers Press
ProLiteracy's Publishing Division
104 Marcellus Street, Syracuse, New York 13204
www.newreaderspress.com

Printed in the United States of America
29

Proceeds from the sale of New Readers Press materials support professional
development, training, and technical assistance programs of ProLiteracy
that benefit local literacy programs in the U.S. and around the globe.

Developmental Editor: Karen Davy
Creative Director: Andrea Woodbury
Art and Design Supervisor: James P. Wallace
Illustrator: Seitu Hayden, represented by Wilkinson Studios Inc.
Production Specialist: Maryellen Casey

Contents

Lesson 1: A Meeting at the Western Hotel 4

Lesson 2: A Helpful Mother-in-Law 10

Lesson 3: A Delayed Flight 16

Lesson 4: Becker's Supermarket 22

Lesson 5: Worried About Her Grandmother 28

Lesson 6: Time for a Pay Raise 34

Lesson 7: A Suit from Drake's 40

Lesson 8: A Loan from Aunt Loretta 46

Lesson 9: A Clothing Donation 52

Lesson 10: A Termite Problem 58

Lesson 11: A Picture of the Eiffel Tower 64

Lesson 12: An Exhausted Student 70

Lesson 13: A Visit to the Metropolitan Museum 76

Lesson 14: Getting Directions 82

Lesson 15: A Jury Summons 88

Listening Exercise Prompts 94

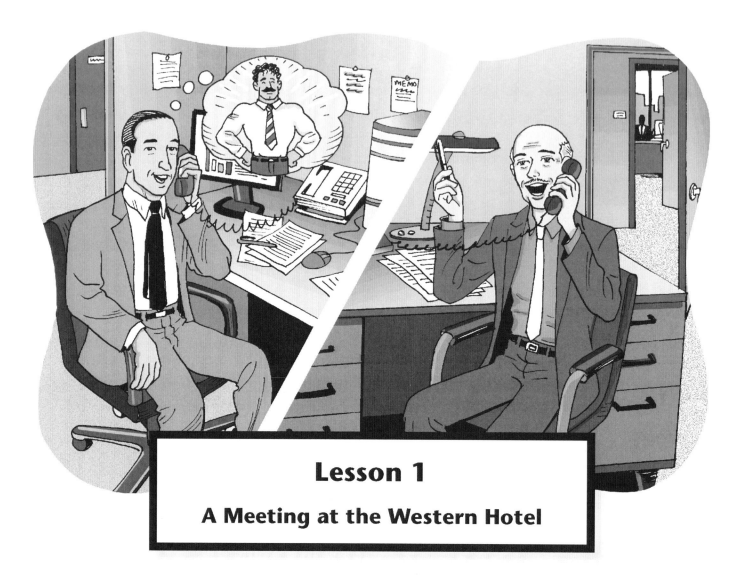

Lesson 1

A Meeting at the Western Hotel

Samir and Conrad work for the same large corporation. But Samir works at the office in Los Angeles, and Conrad works at the office in Chicago. Samir and Conrad never see each other, but they talk on the telephone a few times a week.

Tomorrow Conrad is coming to Los Angeles for a big meeting. Samir is going to meet him in the Western Hotel lobby. "See you tomorrow," says Samir. "But tell me. What do you look like?"

"I'm about 6 feet tall," says Conrad. "I have a lot of hair. It's curly and black. I'm pretty muscular. And I have a mustache."

The next day, Samir arrives at the Western Hotel. He walks into the lobby. There are several people there. But no one looks like Conrad. Then Samir sees a man looking at him. He is about 5 feet 7 inches tall. He is mostly bald. He has a little straight gray hair on the sides. He is very thin and not at all muscular. And he doesn't have a mustache. But then the man approaches him.

"Excuse me," he says. "Are you Samir?"

"Yes, I am," he says. "Conrad? Is that you?"

"Yes!" says Conrad. "It's very nice to meet you." Conrad and Samir shake hands.

"You're a little different from your description," says Samir.

"Oh, right!" says Conrad. "I shaved off my mustache last night."

Answer the questions.

1. What do Samir and Conrad work for?

2. Where does Samir work?

3. Where does Conrad work?

4. How often do Samir and Conrad see each other?

5. When is Conrad coming to Los Angeles for a big meeting?

6. Where is Samir going to meet him?

7. What does Conrad say he looks like?

8. Who is looking at Samir in the hotel lobby?

9. What does he look like?

10. What did Conrad do last night?

Complete the sentences.

is	doesn't have	sees	walks into
looks like	says	approaches	arrives

1. The next day, Samir _____ at the Western Hotel.

2. He _____ the lobby.

3. But no one _____ Conrad.

4. Then Samir _____ a man looking at him.

5. He is about 5 feet 7 inches tall. He _____ mostly bald.

6. And he _____ a mustache.

7. But then the man _____ him.

8. "Excuse me," he _____. "Are you Samir?"

Matching: Definitions

_____ 1. muscular

_____ 2. description

_____ 3. 6 feet

_____ 4. lobby

_____ 5. meeting

_____ 6. mustache

a. an explanation

b. hair that grows above the mouth

c. a large entrance into a hotel or building

d. having strong muscles

e. a time when people get together to talk

f. a height of 72 inches

Talking in the Hotel Lobby

Practice the dialog with a partner.

A. Excuse me. Are you Samir?

B. Yes, I am. Conrad? Is that you?

A. Yes! It's very nice to meet you.

B. It's nice to meet you, too. You're a little different from your description.

A. Oh, right! I shaved off my mustache last night.

B. Yes. That's the difference.

A Better Description

Conrad is a little different from his description. Read the way Conrad describes himself. Then write new sentences about the way he really looks.

Conrad says:

The Way Conrad Really Looks

1. "I'm about 6 feet tall."

    <u>He's about 5 feet 7 inches tall.</u>

2. "I have a lot of hair."

    _____

3. "It's curly and black."

    _____

4. "I'm pretty muscular."

    _____

5. "I have a mustache."

    _____

Listening

Listen. Check (✔) the correct sentence.

1. _____ a. They sometimes see each other.

   _____ b. They don't ever see each other.

2. _____ a. I'm a tall man.

   _____ b. I'm not a tall man.

3. _____ a. I have strong muscles.

   _____ b. I'm very thin.

4. _____ a. My hair is curly and black.

   _____ b. I have hair above my mouth.

5. _____ a. He is a tall man.

   _____ b. He isn't a tall man.

6. _____ a. He has a lot of hair.

   _____ b. He doesn't have much hair.

7. _____ a. He doesn't have hair on his face.

   _____ b. He has hair above his mouth.

8. _____ a. You look the way you said.

   _____ b. You don't look the way you said.

Pronunciation and Writing

Say the words from the story. Write the number of syllables in each word. Underline the stressed syllable.

1. meeting _____

2. telephone _____

3. several _____

4. description _____

5. lobby _____

6. corporation _____

7. mostly _____

8. tomorrow _____

9. office _____

10. mustache _____

11. approaches _____

12. curly _____

13. muscular _____

14. excuse _____

15. different _____

What about you?

Circle _Yes_ or _No_. Then write questions and ask your partner.

Yes   No   1. I work for a large corporation.

Do you work for a large corporation? _____

Yes   No   2. I sometimes talk on the telephone to people I work with.

_____

Yes   No   3. I sometimes go to meetings.

_____

Yes   No   4. I have a lot of hair.

_____

Yes   No   5. I have a mustache.

_____

Topics for Discussion or Writing

1. Do you sometimes talk on the telephone to someone you never see? If so, who is it?
2. What do you look like? Describe yourself.
3. Why do you think Conrad's description is different from the way he really looks?

Lesson 2

A Helpful Mother-in-Law

Jennifer and Shaun are newlyweds. These days, they're both working very long hours. They feel exhausted when they get home at night. Their apartment is a mess. Their laundry basket is full. Their refrigerator is empty. They eat peanut-butter sandwiches for dinner. One evening, Shaun looks at the calendar and says, "My mother is coming on Saturday."

"I remember," says Jennifer. "But it's not a good time. Look at this place!" Jennifer sighs. She doesn't really know her mother-in-law, Evelyn, very well. Evelyn lives 3,000 miles away. Jennifer is happy that Evelyn lives far away. She thinks most mothers-in-law cause problems.

Evelyn arrives on Saturday. She is actually a lovely person and very helpful. When Jennifer and Shaun are at work, Evelyn cleans the apartment. She does the laundry. She shops for food. She cooks delicious meals. One day, Evelyn even paints the living room. Now Jennifer thinks Evelyn is the best mother-in-law in the world.

"Can you stay longer?" asks Jennifer.

"No, I can't," says Evelyn. "I need to go home tomorrow."

"When can you come back?" asks Jennifer.

"Maybe next year," answers Evelyn. "Three thousand miles is a long way. It's very expensive to travel."

"You're right," says Jennifer. Then she turns to Shaun. "We live too far away from your mother. Let's move."

Answer the questions.

1. What are Jennifer and Shaun?

2. How do they feel when they get home at night? Why?

3. How is their apartment?

4. What is full? What is empty?

5. When is Shaun's mother coming?

6. How far away does Evelyn live?

7. What does Jennifer think most mothers-in-law cause?

8. What is Evelyn like?

9. What does Evelyn do when Jennifer and Shaun are at work?

10. What does Jennifer think of Evelyn now?

Complete the sentences.

empty	far away	exhausted	full
helpful	long	best	mess

1. These days, they're both working very _____ hours.

2. They are _____ when they get home in the evening.

3. Their apartment is a _____.

4. Their laundry basket is _____.

5. Their refrigerator is _____.

6. Jennifer is happy that Evelyn lives _____.

7. Evelyn is actually a lovely person and very _____.

8. Now Jennifer thinks Evelyn is the _____ mother-in-law in the world.

Matching: Definitions

_____ 1. meals

_____ 2. calendar

_____ 3. laundry basket

_____ 4. newlyweds

_____ 5. 3,000 miles

_____ 6. mother-in-law

a. the mother of your husband or wife

b. a place to keep clean or dirty clothes

c. a distance of about 4,828 kilometers

d. a chart for the days and months of the year

e. people who recently got married

f. the foods served at breakfast, lunch, and dinner

Talking to Her Mother-in-Law

Practice the dialog with a partner.

A. **You're the best mother-in-law in the world.**

B. Thank you, dear.

A. **Can you stay longer?**

B. No, I can't. I need to go home tomorrow.

A. **When can you come back?**

B. Maybe next year. Three thousand miles is a long way. It's very expensive to travel.

Write new sentences.

It's not a good time for Jennifer and Shaun. But Evelyn is actually a lovely person and very helpful. Read the example. Then write new sentences about what Evelyn does.

Jennifer and Shaun	What does Evelyn do?
1. Their apartment is a mess.	*She cleans the apartment.*
2. Their laundry basket is full.	
3. Their refrigerator is empty.	
4. They eat peanut-butter sandwiches for dinner.	
5. Their living room walls are dirty.	

Listening

Listen. Check (✔) the correct sentence.

1. ____ a. They are working long
        hours.
   ____ b. They recently got married.

2. ____ a. They are very tired.
   ____ b. They are very hungry.

3. ____ a. It's disorganized.
   ____ b. It's neat and clean.

4. ____ a. They eat delicious meals.
   ____ b. They don't eat well.

5. ____ a. She wants Evelyn to come.
   ____ b. She doesn't want Evelyn to
        come.

6. ____ a. She lives far away.
   ____ b. She lives in the same city.

7. ____ a. She causes problems.
   ____ b. She is very helpful.

8. ____ a. She wants her to stay
        longer.
   ____ b. She wants her to go home.

Pronunciation and Writing

Say the words from the story. Write the number of syllables in each word. Underline the stressed syllable.

1. mother-in-law ____

2. laundry ____

3. calendar ____

4. actually ____

5. newlyweds ____

6. travel ____

7. refrigerator ____

8. expensive ____

9. apartment ____

10. sandwiches ____

11. tomorrow ____

12. peanut ____

13. helpful ____

14. exhausted ____

15. thousand ____

What about you?

Circle *Yes* or *No.* Then write questions and ask your partner.

Yes No 1. I feel exhausted when I get home.

<u>Do you feel exhausted when you get home?</u>

Yes No 2. I sometimes eat peanut-butter sandwiches for dinner.

_____

Yes No 3. I have a mother-in-law.

_____

Yes No 4. I think most mothers-in-law cause problems.

_____

Yes No 5. I clean, do laundry, shop, and cook at home.

_____

Topics for Discussion or Writing

1. What things do you need to do at home? Can anyone help you do those things?
2. How far away does your family live? How expensive is it to travel there?
3. Are you sometimes helpful to someone? If so, who do you help and what do you do for that person?

Lesson 3

A Delayed Flight

Jonas is at the airport in Los Angeles. He is very tired after a fifteen-hour flight from Hong Kong. But Jonas still needs to fly home to Atlanta.

Jonas walks toward the gate. He walks quickly because his flight leaves in thirty minutes. At the gate, Jonas looks up at the monitor. His flight, 631, is delayed by an hour. Jonas is disappointed. He really wants to get home. But Jonas goes to an airport restaurant and eats a sandwich. He goes to an airport store and buys a book. Then he returns to his gate.

At the gate, Jonas hears an announcement. His flight is delayed again. This time, it's by forty-five minutes. Jonas is very frustrated, but what can he do? Jonas sits down and opens his book. He reads a few pages, but his eyes feel very heavy. Jonas closes his eyes and falls asleep.

Suddenly, Jonas wakes up and looks around. He looks up at the monitor. Jonas missed his flight! Jonas is very angry at himself.

An airline worker tells Jonas he needs to buy a new ticket to Atlanta. "But don't worry," she says. "There's another flight to Atlanta in about an hour."

"Oh, good," says Jonas.

"Well," she says, "maybe two hours. That flight is delayed."

Answer the questions.

1. Where is Jonas?

2. How many hours was his flight from Hong Kong?

3. Where does Jonas still need to fly?

4. Why does Jonas walk quickly?

5. For how long is his flight, 631, delayed?

6. Where does Jonas go and what does he eat?

7. What does he buy at an airport store?

8. For how long is his flight delayed again?

9. What happens to Jonas after he reads a few pages?

10. What does an airline worker tell Jonas he needs to buy?

Complete the sentences.

ticket	eyes	monitor	flight
book	sandwich	airport	announcement

1. Jonas is at the _____ in Los Angeles.

2. His _____, 631, is delayed by an hour.

3. Jonas goes to an airport restaurant and eats a _____.

4. He goes to an airport store and buys a _____.

5. At the gate, Jonas hears an _____. His flight is delayed again.

6. Jonas closes his _____ and falls asleep.

7. He looks up at the _____. Jonas missed his flight!

8. An airline worker tells Jonas he needs to buy a new _____ to Atlanta.

Matching: Opposites

_____ 1. delayed   a. slowly

_____ 2. quickly   b. calm

_____ 3. frustrated   c. light

_____ 4. tired   d. energetic

_____ 5. disappointed   e. on time

_____ 6. heavy   f. satisfied

Talking to an Airline Worker

Practice the dialog with a partner.

A. I missed Flight 631 to Atlanta.

B. Sorry. You need to buy a new ticket.

A. Is there another flight soon?

B. Don't worry. There's another flight to Atlanta in about an hour.

A. Oh, good.

B. Well, maybe two hours. That flight is delayed.

Check the good ideas.

Your flight is delayed. Check (✔) the things that are good to do. Write other ideas on the lines below.

_____ eat a sandwich

_____ read a book

_____ take another flight

_____ walk around the airport

_____ complain to the airline later

_____ close your eyes and fall asleep

_____ call your family or friends

_____ get angry at an airline worker

_____ buy things at the airport gift shop

_____ ask why the flight is delayed

_____   _____

Listening

Listen. Check (✔) the correct sentence.

1. ____ a. He is in Hong Kong.
   ____ b. He is in Los Angeles.

2. ____ a. It will leave on time.
   ____ b. It will leave one hour later.

3. ____ a. He really wants to get home.
   ____ b. He really wants to eat.

4. ____ a. He listens to a message.
   ____ b. He looks up at the monitor.

5. ____ a. He is tired.
   ____ b. He is hungry.

6. ____ a. He opens his eyes.
   ____ b. He closes his eyes.

7. ____ a. He is on the plane.
   ____ b. The plane left without him.

8. ____ a. His new ticket is free.
   ____ b. He has to pay money for a ticket.

Pronunciation and Writing

Say the words from the story. Write the number of syllables in each word. Underline the stressed syllable.

1. delayed ____

2. monitor ____

3. frustrated ____

4. angry ____

5. asleep ____

6. sandwich ____

7. announcement ____

8. thirty ____

9. disappointed ____

10. returns ____

11. airport ____

12. suddenly ____

13. ticket ____

14. quickly ____

15. another ____

What about you?

Circle *Yes* or *No.* Then write questions and ask your partner.

Yes No   1. I sometimes go to the airport.

Do you sometimes go to the airport?

Yes No   2. I feel tired after a long trip.

_____

Yes No   3. I feel frustrated when my trip is delayed.

_____

Yes No   4. I understand announcements when I hear them.

_____

Yes No   5. I sometimes close my eyes and fall asleep in public places.

_____

Topics for Discussion or Writing

1. Do you sometimes fly on planes? If so, where do you go and how long is the flight?
2. Where do you sometimes hear announcements? What can you do if you don't understand an announcement?
3. For what reasons can flights be delayed?

Lesson 4

Becker's Supermarket

Abby is from a small town, but she lives in a big city now. Every summer, Abby goes home to visit her family. She loves spending time with her family. She also enjoys the delicious meals at home. In Abby's opinion, the food is much better there. Her family has a garden. Her father catches fish in the lake. Her mother bakes fresh pies.

Abby thinks the food in the city is terrible. For example, in Abby's neighborhood, there is a Becker's Supermarket. There are Becker's Supermarkets all over her city. Abby doesn't like shopping at Becker's. At Becker's, there are too many processed foods: canned, frozen, refrigerated, and dehydrated. Their foods have too many artificial ingredients: sweeteners, flavorings, dyes, and preservatives. Even Becker's fresh foods don't taste very good. But Abby needs to eat, so she usually shops at Becker's.

In July, Abby goes home for a visit. On her first night home, her mother serves a delicious dinner of vegetables and fish. She serves a peach pie for dessert. "Yum!" says Abby to her mother. "I miss this so much. You can't eat like this in the city, Mom."

"I'm glad you like it," says her mother. "But I didn't have a lot of time to cook today. I bought everything at the new Becker's Supermarket."

Answer the questions.

1. Where is Abby from? Where does she live now?

2. When does she go home to visit her family?

3. What does she enjoy at home?

4. What does her father catch in the lake? What does her mother bake?

5. What does Abby think about the food in the city?

6. Where are there Becker's Supermarkets?

7. What kinds of processed foods are there?

8. What kinds of artificial ingredients do they have?

9. What does Abby's mother serve for dinner and dessert?

10. Where did she buy everything?

What is the category?

sweeteners	apple	frozen	dehydrated
peach	dyes	cherry	pumpkin
refrigerated	canned	flavorings	preservatives

Kinds of Pies	Artificial Ingredients	Ways Foods Are Processed
1. _____	1. _____	1. _____
2. _____	2. _____	2. _____
3. _____	3. _____	3. _____
4. _____	4. _____	4. _____

Matching: Definitions

_____ 1. sweeteners   a. preserved by freezing

_____ 2. dehydrated   b. things put into foods and drinks to change the colors

_____ 3. frozen   c. chilled or cooled

_____ 4. dyes   d. dried out; with water removed

_____ 5. refrigerated   e. things put into foods to make them last a long time

_____ 6. preservatives   f. things put into foods or drinks to make them taste sweet

Talking About Dinner

Practice the dialog with a partner.

A. Yum! I miss this so much.

B. Really?

A. Yes! You can't eat like this in the city.

B. I'm glad you like it.

A. I love it!

B. Well, I didn't have a lot of time to cook today. I bought everything at the new Becker's Supermarket.

Matching

Match the words and pictures of the processed foods. Write the words on the lines below.

canned	frozen	dehydrated

1. _____   2. _____   3. _____

Listening

Listen. Check (✔) the correct sentence.

1. _____ a. She goes in January.
   _____ b. She goes in July.

2. _____ a. Their food is fresh.
   _____ b. Their food is processed.

3. _____ a. It doesn't taste good.
   _____ b. It tastes good.

4. _____ a. There is only one in her city.
   _____ b. There are many in her city.

5. _____ a. The foods are canned and frozen.
   _____ b. The foods are delicious.

6. _____ a. They have fresh vegetables.
   _____ b. They have dyes and preservatives.

7. _____ a. Abby never shops at Becker's.
   _____ b. Abby often shops at Becker's.

8. _____ a. Becker's has good food.
   _____ b. Becker's doesn't have good food.

Pronunciation and Writing

Say the words from the story. Write the number of syllables in each word. Underline the stressed syllable.

1. artificial _____
2. shopping _____
3. refrigerated _____
4. neighborhood _____
5. preservatives _____

6. everything _____
7. ingredients _____
8. dessert _____
9. frozen _____
10. sweeteners _____

11. processed _____
12. flavorings _____
13. supermarket _____
14. dehydrated _____
15. city _____

What about you?

Circle *Yes* or *No*. Then write questions and ask your partner.

Yes No 1. I live in a big city now.

<u>Do you live in a big city now?</u>

Yes No 2. I think the food in the city is terrible.

_____

Yes No 3. I sometimes eat processed foods.

_____

Yes No 4. I sometimes eat foods with artificial ingredients.

_____

Yes No 5. I usually shop at a large supermarket.

_____

Topics for Discussion or Writing

1. Where do you usually shop? How are the foods there?
2. Where can you shop for foods without artificial ingredients in your area?
3. Do you think the food is better in the U.S. or in your native country? Why do you think that?

Lesson 5

Worried About Her Grandmother

Mireya lives with her grandmother, Dolores. Dolores is 85 years old, and Mireya loves her very much. And fortunately, Dolores is in very good condition for her age.

One morning, Dolores walks into the kitchen. "I didn't sleep last night," she says. "A crazy woman was dancing on the neighbor's roof."

"Really?" asks Mireya. But Mireya thinks her grandmother's comment is very strange. After all, some elderly people have dementia. They can't concentrate. They can't remember things. They feel confused. Sometimes they have hallucinations, or see and hear things that aren't there. Mireya feels very worried.

Mireya takes Dolores to the doctor. The doctor orders several tests for Dolores. She has an MRI (Magnetic Resonance Imaging) scan of her brain. She has some laboratory tests. The doctor does an evaluation. He checks her memory, language, and other things.

Soon, Mireya learns that the test results are good. The doctor doesn't think Dolores has dementia. Sometimes Dolores still talks about the crazy woman dancing on the roof. But Mireya tries not to worry about it.

One day, Mireya and Dolores go outside. Their neighbor, Mrs. Lang, is picking up her newspaper. "Hello!" says Mrs. Lang. "I hope I'm not keeping you awake at night. I'm taking a dance class. And since it's so hot in the house, I like to practice on the roof."

Answer the questions.

1. Who does Mireya live with? How old is she?

2. How is Dolores for her age?

3. What does Dolores say a crazy woman was doing?

4. What do some elderly people have?

5. What can't they do? How do they feel?

6. What do they sometimes have?

7. Where does Mireya take Dolores?

8. What tests does Dolores have?

9. What does the doctor do? What does he check?

10. How are the test results?

Complete the sentences.

| MRI | hallucinations | test results | comment |
| doctor | language | dementia | laboratory tests |

1. Mireya thinks her grandmother's _____ is very strange.

2. After all, some elderly people have _____.

3. Sometimes they have _____, or see and hear things that aren't there.

4. The _____ orders several tests for Dolores.

5. She has an _____ (Magnetic Resonance Imaging) scan of her brain.

6. She has some _____.

7. The doctor checks her memory, _____, and other things.

8. Soon, Mireya learns that the _____ are good.

Matching: Definitions

_____ 1. strange   a. unable to think clearly

_____ 2. awake   b. older

_____ 3. worried   c. anxious or nervous

_____ 4. confused   d. odd or unusual

_____ 5. elderly   e. not asleep

Talking to the Doctor

Practice the dialog with a partner.

A. I'm worried about my grandmother.

B. Why are you worried?

A. I think she's having hallucinations.

B. How old is your grandmother?

A. She's 85 years old.

B. Please bring her in. We'll do some tests.

Matching

Match the words and pictures of the tests Dolores has. Write the words on the lines below.

MRI	laboratory test	evaluation

1. _____   2. _____   3. _____

Listening

Listen. Check (✔) the correct sentence.

1. ____ a. Her health is good.

   ____ b. She has many health problems.

2. ____ a. She doesn't think it happened.

   ____ b. She saw the crazy woman, too.

3. ____ a. They can't dance.

   ____ b. They have hallucinations.

4. ____ a. She can't concentrate.

   ____ b. She feels very worried.

5. ____ a. She takes medication.

   ____ b. She has a scan of her brain.

6. ____ a. He checks her roof.

   ____ b. He checks her memory.

7. ____ a. Dolores has dementia.

   ____ b. Dolores doesn't have dementia.

8. ____ a. She is dancing on the roof at night.

   ____ b. She sees things that aren't there.

Pronunciation and Writing

Say the words from the story. Write the number of syllables in each word. Underline the stressed syllable.

1. laboratory ____

2. language ____

3. condition ____

4. memory ____

5. dementia ____

6. comment ____

7. hallucinations ____

8. concentrate ____

9. imaging ____

10. magnetic ____

11. remember ____

12. evaluation ____

13. fortunately ____

14. grandmother ____

15. results ____

What about you?

Circle *Yes* or *No.* Then write questions and ask your partner.

Yes   No   1.   I live with my grandmother.

Do you live with your grandmother? _____

Yes   No   2.   I know a person who has dementia.

_____

Yes   No   3.   I sometimes help an elderly person.

_____

Yes   No   4.   I sometimes have an MRI.

_____

Yes   No   5.   I sometimes have laboratory tests.

_____

Topics for Discussion or Writing

1. What problems can a person with dementia have?
2. What other problems can elderly people sometimes have?
3. What kinds of medical tests do doctors sometimes order?

Lesson 6

Time for a Pay Raise

Graciela does janitorial work. Five nights a week, Graciela and several other workers clean three floors of a large office building. It's hard work, but Graciela does her job very well. Last year, she received an excellent performance evaluation and two pay raises.

Recently, the janitorial services company hired Rogelio. The supervisor asked Graciela to train him. "You're a wonderful worker," said the supervisor. "Can you please show Rogelio what to do?" Now, Graciela and Rogelio are working together. Unfortunately, Rogelio isn't a very good worker. He's often late. He takes too many breaks. And he doesn't clean carefully.

Right now, Graciela and Rogelio are in an office on the 21st floor. Graciela is vacuuming the carpet. Rogelio is sitting down in an office chair, admiring the city lights outside. "So," Rogelio yells, "I've worked here for three weeks now. Do you think it's time to ask for a pay raise?"

Graciela turns off her vacuum. Then she gives Rogelio a long look. "You need to work for at least three months before you're eligible for a pay raise. And I have to be honest with you, Rogelio. At this point, you really don't deserve one."

"Maybe you're right," says Rogelio. "But can you recommend me for a management position?"

Answer the questions.

1. What kind of work does Graciela do?

2. What do she and several other workers clean five nights a week?

3. How does Graciela do her job?

4. What did she receive last year?

5. Who did the janitorial services company recently hire?

6. Who asked Graciela to train him?

7. What kind of worker is Rogelio? What does he do?

8. What is Graciela doing on the 21st floor?

9. What is Rogelio doing?

10. For how long does Rogelio need to work before he is eligible for a pay raise?

Complete the sentences.

pay raise	company	floor	office chair
worker	months	carpet	supervisor

1. Recently, the janitorial services _____ hired Rogelio.

2. The _____ asked Graciela to train him.

3. Unfortunately, Rogelio isn't a very good _____.

4. Right now, Graciela and Rogelio are in an office on the 21st _____.

5. Graciela is vacuuming the _____.

6. Rogelio is sitting down in an _____, admiring the city lights outside.

7. Rogelio yells, "Do you think it's time to ask for a _____?"

8. Graciela tells him he needs to work for at least three _____.

Matching: Definitions

_____ 1. deserve   a. to give someone a job

_____ 2. recommend   b. to look at something or someone with pleasure

_____ 3. admire   c. to earn something good

_____ 4. clean   d. to show someone how to do a job

_____ 5. hire   e. to say someone or something is good

_____ 6. train   f. to remove dirt from things; to wash

Talking About a Pay Raise

Practice the dialog with a partner.

A. I've worked here for three weeks now.

B. Good for you.

A. Do you think it's time to ask for a pay raise?

B. You need to work for at least three months before you're eligible for a pay raise.

A. Three months?

B. Yes. And I have to be honest with you. At this point, you really don't deserve one.

A. But can you recommend me for a management position?

Check the good ideas.

You want to be a good worker. Check (✔) the things that are good to do. Write other ideas on the lines below.

_____ do your job very well

_____ arrive late

_____ take too many breaks

_____ work quickly

_____ call in sick often

_____ ask for a pay raise often

_____ ask about a management position

_____ show other workers what to do

_____ ask for a performance evaluation

_____ sit down a lot at work

_____   _____

Listening

Listen. Check (✔) the correct sentence.

1. _____ a. She does janitorial work.

   _____ b. She has a management position.

2. _____ a. She isn't a very good worker.

   _____ b. She does her job very well.

3. _____ a. She shows him what to do.

   _____ b. She hires him.

4. _____ a. He cleans carefully.

   _____ b. He is often late.

5. _____ a. He vacuums the carpet.

   _____ b. He sits down a lot.

6. _____ a. He wants more money.

   _____ b. He doesn't want her to train him.

7. _____ a. He can ask the supervisor.

   _____ b. He can't get a pay raise yet.

8. _____ a. He isn't a good worker.

   _____ b. He isn't a good supervisor.

Pronunciation and Writing

Say the words from the story. Write the number of syllables in each word. Underline the stressed syllable.

1. recommend _____
2. raises _____
3. building _____
4. honest _____
5. janitorial _____

6. excellent _____
7. admiring _____
8. evaluation _____
9. deserve _____
10. wonderful _____

11. performance _____
12. carefully _____
13. eligible _____
14. vacuuming _____
15. carpet _____

What about you?

Circle *Yes* or *No*. Then write questions and ask your partner.

Yes   No   1.   I do janitorial work.

Do you do janitorial work?

Yes   No   2.   I sometimes show other workers what to do.

_____

Yes   No   3.   I work with someone who isn't a good worker.

_____

Yes   No   4.   I sometimes receive performance evaluations.

_____

Yes   No   5.   I sometimes ask for a pay raise.

_____

Topics for Discussion or Writing

1.   Do you have a job? If so, what do you do?
2.   For what reasons do workers get pay raises?
3.   How do you think workers get management positions?

Lesson 7

A Suit from Drake's

Shirin is in a dressing room at Drake's Department Store. She is trying on a pair of black dress pants. They fit very well, but before she takes them off, the salesclerk brings in a matching jacket. She also has a pretty pink blouse. The salesclerk is very persuasive. "Beautiful!" says the salesclerk. "You look very professional in a suit!" Shirin smiles in front of the big mirror.

"Why not?" she says. "I'll take it all!"

At home, Shirin looks in her bag and sighs. She really regrets spending so much money. After all, Shirin is a nurse in a big hospital. She wears a uniform at work. She doesn't need a suit. And she certainly doesn't need to spend more money this month.

The next day, Shirin returns the jacket and blouse to Drake's. "Can I show you something else?" asks the salesclerk. "Or would you like a store credit to buy something later?"

"No, thank you," says Shirin firmly. "Just a refund, please."

When Shirin gets home that evening, there is a message on her answering machine. It's from her boss at the hospital. "Hi, Shirin," she says. "We have an opening for a nursing director. Can you come in for an interview on Monday? Oh, and it's a good idea to wear a suit."

Answer the questions.

1. Where is Shirin?

2. What is she trying on?

3. What does the salesclerk bring in?

4. What is the salesclerk like?

5. What does Shirin do when she looks in her bag at home?

6. What does she really regret?

7. What is Shirin's occupation? What does she wear at work?

8. What does Shirin do the next day?

9. Who is the message on her answering machine from?

10. What job is there an opening for?

Complete the sentences.

mirror	salesclerk	bag	dressing room
blouse	money	pants	suit

1. Shirin is in a _____ at Drake's Department Store.

2. She is trying on a pair of black dress _____.

3. But before she takes them off, the _____ brings in a matching jacket.

4. She also has a pretty pink _____.

5. "You look very professional in a _____!" says the salesclerk.

6. Shirin smiles in front of the big _____.

7. At home, Shirin looks in her _____ and sighs.

8. She really regrets spending so much _____.

Matching: Definitions

_____ 1. uniform
_____ 2. opening
_____ 3. refund
_____ 4. nurse
_____ 5. store credit
_____ 6. boss

a. the money returned for something you bought

b. a supervisor; a person in charge of others

c. money you can spend in a particular store

d. a job or position that is available

e. special clothing you wear at some jobs

f. a person who takes care of sick people

Talking to a Salesclerk

Practice the dialog with a partner.

A. **I want to return this jacket and blouse.**

B. Do you have the receipt?

A. **Yes. Here it is.**

B. Can I show you something else?

A. **I don't think so.**

B. Or would you like a store credit to buy something later?

A. **No, thank you. Just a refund, please.**

Check the good ideas.

You regret spending money for clothes you don't really need. Check (✔) the things that are good to do. Write other ideas on the lines below.

_____ wear them a few times

_____ return them

_____ look in the bag and sigh

_____ sell them at a yard sale

_____ exchange them for clothes you can wear often

_____ get a store credit for them

_____ hang them in your closet for the future

_____ get a refund for them

_____ throw away the receipt

_____ give them to someone who needs them

_____   _____

Listening

Listen. Check (✔) the correct sentence.

1. _____ a. The jacket is pink.

   _____ b. The jacket is black.

2. _____ a. She wants Shirin to spend money.

   _____ b. She wants Shirin to return things.

3. _____ a. Shirin buys only the pants.

   _____ b. Shirin buys everything.

4. _____ a. She wants another suit.

   _____ b. She regrets spending the money.

5. _____ a. She wears a uniform at work.

   _____ b. She wears a suit at work.

6. _____ a. She takes them back to the store.

   _____ b. She tries them on at the store.

7. _____ a. She wants a store credit.

   _____ b. She wants her money back.

8. _____ a. It's from her boss at the hospital.

   _____ b. It's from the salesclerk at Drake's.

Pronunciation and Writing

Say the words from the story. Write the number of syllables in each word. Underline the stressed syllable.

1. mirror _____

2. uniform _____

3. refund _____

4. interview _____

5. opening _____

6. salesclerk _____

7. matching _____

8. persuasive _____

9. regrets _____

10. returns _____

11. director _____

12. certainly _____

13. jacket _____

14. hospital _____

15. nursing _____

What about you?

Circle *Yes* or *No.* Then write questions and ask your partner.

Yes   No   1. I sometimes wear a suit.

   Do you sometimes wear a suit?

Yes   No   2. I usually wear a uniform.

   _____

Yes   No   3. I think some salesclerks are very persuasive.

   _____

Yes   No   4. I sometimes regret spending money on clothes.

   _____

Yes   No   5. I sometimes ask for a refund.

   _____

Topics for Discussion or Writing

1. Do you sometimes return clothing to a department store? If so, why do you return it?
2. What kinds of clothing do you wear for a job interview? What kinds of clothing do you wear at work?
3. What do salesclerks sometimes say to be persuasive?

Lesson 8

A Loan from Aunt Loretta

Loretta is very careful with her money. She pays her bills on time and rarely spends money on things for herself. But Loretta is also very generous and sometimes helps people in her family. Right now, Loretta is very worried about her nephew, Charlie. Charlie called her last night. It seems he needs money for a medical procedure.

Unfortunately, Charlie doesn't qualify for a bank loan. He doesn't have a job right now. And his credit history isn't very good. Loretta thinks Charlie probably makes bad decisions about money. Still, Loretta wants to help him if she can.

At three o'clock, Loretta's doorbell rings. It's Charlie, and he looks very sad. Loretta is sure that his health problem is serious, but she doesn't want to ask too many questions. "How much do you need?" Loretta asks Charlie.

"I think the transplant costs about $10,000," says Charlie.

"A transplant!" Loretta thinks. "Is it his heart? Is it his liver or a kidney?" Loretta gets out her checkbook.

"This is a loan," says Charlie. "I'll pay you back, I promise. Every month, you'll get a payment with interest."

"Please don't worry about that now," says Loretta. "Your health is more important than money. But tell me, what kind of transplant do you need?"

"Oh, Aunt Loretta," whispers Charlie. "It's a hair transplant."

Answer the questions.

1. When does Loretta pay her bills?

2. How often does she spend money on things for herself?

3. Who is Loretta worried about right now?

4. What does it seem Charlie needs money for?

5. What doesn't Charlie qualify for?

6. How is Charlie's credit history?

7. What time does Loretta's doorbell ring?

8. What doesn't Loretta want to ask?

9. How much does Charlie think the transplant costs?

10. What kind of transplant does Charlie need?

Complete the sentences.

decisions	transplant	credit history	medical procedure
bank loan	nephew	job	health problem

1. Right now, Loretta is very worried about her _____, Charlie.

2. It seems he needs money for a _____.

3. Unfortunately, Charlie doesn't qualify for a _____.

4. He doesn't have a _____ right now.

5. And his _____ isn't very good.

6. Loretta thinks Charlie probably makes bad _____ about money.

7. Loretta is sure that his _____ is serious.

8. "I think the _____ costs about $10,000," says Charlie.

Matching: Definitions

_____ 1. payment   a. papers that tell how much money you owe

_____ 2. bills   b. the percentage of money you pay back with a loan

_____ 3. loan   c. a small book of bank forms you use to pay for things

_____ 4. interest   d. your record of borrowing and paying back

_____ 5. checkbook   e. money that you borrow and later pay back

_____ 6. credit history f. the money you give to pay for something

Talking About a Loan

Practice the dialog with a partner.

A. How much do you need?

B. I think the transplant costs about $10,000.

A. Oh, dear.

B. This is a loan. I'll pay you back, I promise.

A. Please don't worry about that now.

B. Every month, you'll get a payment with interest.

A. Your health is more important than money.

Check the good ideas.

Your nephew needs money for a medical procedure. Check (✔) the things that are good to do. Write other ideas on the lines below.

_____ write him a check

_____ give him a few dollars

_____ don't answer the doorbell

_____ tell him to get a bank loan

_____ tell him he makes bad decisions about money

_____ tell him to get a job

_____ ask what kind of procedure he needs

_____ ask if his health problem is serious

_____ lend him the money, with interest

_____ tell him to ask other relatives for the money

_____   _____

Listening

Listen. Check (✔) the correct sentence.

1. _____ a. She makes bad decisions.

   _____ b. She is very careful with her money.

2. _____ a. She looks very sad.

   _____ b. She helps people in her family.

3. _____ a. He needs a medical procedure.

   _____ b. He doesn't have a lot of hair.

4. _____ a. His credit history isn't very good.

   _____ b. He has a good job.

5. _____ a. He needs to pay his bills on time.

   _____ b. He needs an expensive body part.

6. _____ a. Does he need this to live?

   _____ b. Does he need this to look better?

7. _____ a. She wants to give him the money.

   _____ b. She wants him to pay her back.

8. _____ a. He'll pay more than he borrows.

   _____ b. He doesn't want her money.

Pronunciation and Writing

Say the words from the story. Write the number of syllables in each word. Underline the stressed syllable.

1. qualify _____
2. medical _____
3. checkbook _____
4. interest _____
5. nephew _____
6. history _____
7. generous _____
8. procedure _____
9. whispers _____
10. decisions _____
11. transplant _____
12. unfortunately _____
13. payment _____
14. rarely _____
15. kidney _____

50   Lesson 8   A Loan from Aunt Loretta

What about you?

Circle *Yes* or *No*. Then write questions and ask your partner.

Yes No   1. I pay my bills on time.

Do you pay your bills on time? _____

Yes No   2. I rarely spend money on things for myself.

_____

Yes No   3. I sometimes help people in my family.

_____

Yes No   4. I sometimes make bad decisions about money.

_____

Yes No   5. I sometimes need money for a medical procedure.

_____

Topics for Discussion or Writing

1. Are you careful with your money? If so, what do you do?
2. When do people ask for bank loans?
3. What kinds of medical procedures can people have? How do they pay for them?

Lesson 9

A Clothing Donation

Midori opens her bedroom closet and puts several pieces of clothing in a large plastic bag: a dress, three blouses, two skirts, and a pair of pants. Then she looks at her husband's clothes. Midori sees Kano's old brown jacket. It's still in good condition. But Midori doesn't like the way Kano looks in this jacket. Besides, Midori bought him a new gray jacket last year. So, Midori puts Kano's brown jacket in the bag. Then she drops off the bag at the thrift store.

The thrift store resells clothing and other usable items. Then they use the money for charity. This charity helps many people. Midori always feels good about donating things she doesn't need.

Two weeks later, Kano opens his closet. "Hmm," he says. "I can't find my brown jacket."

"Oh," says Midori. "I donated it to the thrift store."

"Really?" asks Kano. "But I liked that jacket."

"Well," says Midori, "it's for a good cause. I'm trying to help a great charity. And you have your gray jacket."

The next day, Kano comes home with a shopping bag. "What's in the bag?" asks Midori.

"Oh," says Kano. "I did two things to help a great charity. I went to the thrift store and bought my old brown jacket. Then I donated my gray one."

Answer the questions.

1. What pieces of her clothing does Midori put in a large plastic bag?

2. How is Kano's old brown jacket? What doesn't Midori like about it?

3. What did Midori buy Kano last year?

4. Where does Midori put Kano's brown jacket? Where does she drop off the bag?

5. What does the thrift store resell?

6. What do they use the money for? Who does it help?

7. How does Midori feel about donating things she doesn't need?

8. Two weeks later, what does Kano say when he opens his closet?

9. The next day, what does Kano come home with?

10. What did he buy? What did he donate?

Complete the sentences.

resells	use	feels good	helps
puts	sees	doesn't like	drops off

1. Midori _____ Kano's old brown jacket.

2. Midori _____ the way Kano looks in this jacket.

3. So, Midori _____ Kano's brown jacket in the bag.

4. Then she _____ the bag at the thrift store.

5. The thrift store _____ clothing and other usable items.

6. Then they _____ the money for charity.

7. This charity _____ many people.

8. Midori always _____ about donating things she doesn't need.

Matching: Definitions

_____ 1. jacket

_____ 2. closet

_____ 3. thrift store

_____ 4. charity

_____ 5. items

_____ 6. clothing

a. a business that resells usable items for charity

b. clothes; things you wear on your body

c. things

d. a short coat you wear to stay warm

e. a place at home to hang your clothing

f. an organization that supports people in need

Talking at Home

Practice the dialog with a partner.

A. Hmm. I can't find my brown jacket.

B. Oh. I donated it to the thrift store.

A. Really? But I liked that jacket.

B. Well, it's for a good cause. I'm trying to help a great charity.

A. Which thrift store did you take it to?

B. I took it to the one on 5th Avenue.

Checklist

You're trying to help a charity. Check (✔) the things that you can donate. Write other ideas on the lines below.

_____ clothing	_____ money	_____ pots and pans
_____ blankets	_____ appliances	_____ books
_____ a TV	_____ school supplies	_____ a car
_____ food	_____ a computer	_____ videos
_____ furniture	_____ jewelry	_____ baby things
_____	_____	_____

Listening

Listen. Check (✔) the correct sentence.

1. ____ a. It looks terrible.

    ____ b. It's still in good condition.

2. ____ a. Kano needs a new jacket.

    ____ b. Kano has two jackets right now.

3. ____ a. She leaves the bag there.

    ____ b. She opens the bag there.

4. ____ a. They sell your things again.

    ____ b. You sell your things to them.

5. ____ a. They give jackets to people.

    ____ b. They support people in need.

6. ____ a. She likes to help people.

    ____ b. She likes to buy new clothes.

7. ____ a. He needs a new brown jacket.

    ____ b. His brown jacket isn't there.

8. ____ a. He has his old brown jacket.

    ____ b. He has his new gray jacket.

Pronunciation and Writing

Say the words from the story. Write the number of syllables in each word. Underline the stressed syllable.

1. bedroom ____

2. blouses ____

3. several ____

4. shopping ____

5. plastic ____

6. jacket ____

7. donating ____

8. husband's ____

9. condition ____

10. closet ____

11. usable ____

12. besides ____

13. charity ____

14. clothing ____

15. pieces ____

What about you?

Circle *Yes* or *No*. Then write questions and ask your partner.

Yes   No   1.   I have some old clothing in my closet.

Do you have some old clothing in your closet?

Yes   No   2.   I sometimes donate my old clothing.

_____

Yes   No   3.   I sometimes donate other usable items.

_____

Yes   No   4.   I sometimes buy things at a thrift store.

_____

Yes   No   5.   I sometimes try to help a charity.

_____

Topics for Discussion or Writing

1. Is there a thrift store in your community? If so, where is it and what can you buy there?
2. What are some charities you know about?
3. How do charities sometimes help people?

Lesson 10

A Termite Problem

Magda's apartment building has termites. She knows that termites eat wood and cause serious damage. Magda sees the holes in her wood floor. She sees holes in the wood door. She sees holes in the wood around her windows. Sometimes she even sees termites in her apartment. And that's the worst thing because Magda really hates bugs.

Magda's landlord decides to fumigate the entire apartment complex. Magda is happy the landlord is doing something. But the fumigation is a little inconvenient. Magda has a lot to do. She needs to put some of her foods, drinks, and medicines in special bags. She needs to remove her plants. And she needs to move out of her apartment and stay at a hotel for two days. Magda's landlord gives Magda and the other tenants an allowance, so they don't have to pay for their hotel rooms.

On Tuesday, Magda checks into the Vacation Inn. Her room is very nice. There are no holes in the floor, in the door, or around the windows. She doesn't see any termites. This place is great.

Magda decides to take a walk. She goes down to the lobby. Magda sees one of the other tenants, Mr. Foster. "It's so nice to be away from the bugs!" says Magda.

"But don't go outside," says Mr. Foster. "There are mosquitoes everywhere!"

Answer the questions.

1. What does Magda's apartment building have?

2. What do termites eat? What do they cause?

3. Where does Magda see holes?

4. What does Magda really hate?

5. What does Magda's landlord decide to do?

6. What does Magda need to put in special bags?

7. What does she need to remove?

8. For how long does she need to stay at a hotel?

9. When does Magda check into the Vacation Inn? How is her room?

10. Who does Magda see in the lobby? What does he say?

Complete the sentences.

medicines	fumigation	termites	apartment
holes	wood	windows	landlord

1. Magda's apartment building has _____.

2. She knows that termites eat _____ and cause serious damage.

3. Magda sees the _____ in her wood floor.

4. She sees holes in the wood around her _____.

5. Magda's _____ decides to fumigate the entire apartment complex.

6. But the _____ is a little inconvenient.

7. She needs to put some of her foods, drinks, and _____ in special bags.

8. And she needs to move out of her _____ and stay at a hotel.

Matching: Definitions

_____ 1. allowance   a. another word for *insects*

_____ 2. tenants   b. insects that suck blood and can transmit diseases

_____ 3. damage   c. money to cover expenses

_____ 4. termites   d. insects that live in colonies and eat wood

_____ 5. bugs   e. the people who rent apartments

_____ 6. mosquitoes   f. the harmful effect on something

Talking About Fumigation

Practice the dialog with a partner.

A. What do I need to do before the fumigation?

B. You need to put some of your foods, drinks, and medicines in special bags.

A. What about my plants?

B. You'll need to remove them.

A. For how long do we need to move out?

B. Just for a couple of days. But the landlord is giving us an allowance, so we don't have to pay for our hotel rooms.

Check the good ideas.

You have termites in your home. Check (✔) the things that are good to do. Write other ideas on the lines below.

_____ notify the landlord

_____ spray insecticide

_____ fill in the holes

_____ fumigate your home

_____ discuss it with the other tenants or neighbors

_____ move to another home

_____ stay at a hotel for a long time

_____ ignore them; termites can't hurt you

_____ fill in the holes around your home

_____ buy new floors, doors, and windows

_____

_____

Listening

Listen. Check (✔) the correct sentence.

1. ____ a. They eat wood.

   ____ b. They can transmit diseases.

2. ____ a. Everyone is happy.

   ____ b. Everyone needs to move
   out.

3. ____ a. Magda has a lot to do.

   ____ b. Magda really hates bugs.

4. ____ a. She needs to take them out.

   ____ b. She needs to put them in
   bags.

5. ____ a. She needs to find a new
   apartment.

   ____ b. She needs to leave her
   apartment.

6. ____ a. Their hotel rooms are free.

   ____ b. Their hotel rooms are half-
   price.

7. ____ a. Her room is very nice.

   ____ b. Her room has termites, too.

8. ____ a. There are termites outside.

   ____ b. There are mosquitoes outside.

Pronunciation and Writing

Say the words from the story. Write the number of syllables in each word. Underline the stressed syllable.

1. termites ____

2. tenants ____

3. damage ____

4. entire ____

5. building ____

6. lobby ____

7. fumigate ____

8. complex ____

9. allowance ____

10. landlord ____

11. inconvenient ____

12. mosquitoes ____

13. special ____

14. remove ____

15. fumigation ____

What about you?

Circle *Yes* or *No*. Then write questions and ask your partner.

Yes **No**   1. I have termites in my home.

Do you have termites in your home?

Yes **No**   2. I see holes from termites around my home.

_____

Yes **No**   3. I really hate bugs.

_____

Yes **No**   4. I sometimes check into a hotel.

_____

Yes **No**   5. I sometimes take a walk.

_____

Topics for Discussion or Writing

1. What bugs can cause damage or bother you at home?
2. What things do landlords need to do to take care of their property?
3. What things do people need to do before they fumigate?

Lesson 11

A Picture of the Eiffel Tower

Philip and his co-worker Owen are on a four-day business trip to Paris, France. Philip and Owen are very excited to be in Paris, but they don't have a lot of free time. On their last day, Philip and Owen decide they can spend a few hours sightseeing. "We're in Paris," says Owen. "Let's see *something!*"

Philip and Owen take a taxi to the Eiffel Tower, a famous landmark in Paris. Philip admires it very much. "I want to take a picture of this," says Philip, "and send it to my mother in California." Unfortunately, Philip doesn't have a camera. Philip thinks for a moment. "Maybe I can go to a store and buy a cheap digital camera," he says. "Then I can come back and take a picture of the Eiffel Tower. Then I can go back to the hotel and call my mother for her e-mail address. Then I can go to an Internet café. And then I can use a computer to send her the photo of the Eiffel Tower. My mother will love that!" he says.

Philip looks at his watch. "If I hurry," he says, "I can make it!"

"Or," says Owen, "you can buy your mother a postcard. Then you can put a stamp on it and mail it to her. And then we can see more of Paris."

Answer the questions.

1. Where are Philip and his co-worker Owen on a four-day business trip to?

2. What don't Philip and Owen have a lot of?

3. On their last day, what do they decide they can do?

4. Where do Philip and Owen take a taxi to?

5. What does Philip want to do? Where does he want to send it?

6. Unfortunately, what doesn't Philip have?

7. Where can he go? What can he buy?

8. What can he call his mother for?

9. Where can he use a computer to send her the photo?

10. What does Owen say Philip can do?

Complete the sentences.

camera	computer	Eiffel Tower	e-mail address
store	picture	Internet café	landmark

1. Philip and Owen take a taxi to the Eiffel Tower, a famous _____ in Paris.

2. "I want to take a _____ of this," says Philip.

3. Unfortunately, Philip doesn't have a _____.

4. "Maybe I can go to a _____ and buy a cheap digital camera."

5. "Then I can come back and take a picture of the _____."

6. "Then I can go back to the hotel and call my mother for her _____."

7. "Then I can go to an _____."

8. "And then I can use a _____ to send her the photo of the Eiffel Tower."

Matching: Definitions

_____ 1. postcard

_____ 2. business trip

_____ 3. stamp

_____ 4. free time

_____ 5. sightseeing

_____ 6. Paris

a. a small paper you put on mail that shows the postage

b. recreation; time off

c. a card you can mail with a picture on one side

d. the capital of France

e. travel for work

f. the act of visiting interesting places

Talking at the Eiffel Tower

Practice the dialog with a partner.

A. **I want to take a picture of this.**

B. Unfortunately, you don't have a camera.

A. **Maybe I can buy a cheap digital camera. Then I can come back and take a picture.**

B. I have a better idea.

A. **What's that?**

B. Why don't you buy a postcard? Then we can do more sightseeing.

Philip's Postcard

Read Philip's postcard from Paris. Then answer the questions.

Dear Mom,

Greetings from the Eiffel Tower!
Sorry this is just a postcard,
but I don't have my camera. My
co-worker and I are spending a few
hours sightseeing. We're also going
to the Louvre Museum and the Arc
de Triomphe. I'll call you when I get
home—probably before you get this
postcard.

Love,
Philip

0,85 €   FRANCE

Mrs. Laura Ashford
4982 Field Street
Sacramento, CA 01234
USA

1. What are Philip and his co-worker spending a few hours doing?

2. Where are they also going?

3. When will Philip call his mother?

Listening

Listen. Check (✔) the correct sentence.

1. _____ a. They're on vacation.

   _____ b. They're traveling for work.

2. _____ a. They want to sit in the hotel.

   _____ b. They want to see interesting places.

3. _____ a. It's a famous landmark in Paris.

   _____ b. It's an Internet café.

4. _____ a. He wants to take a photo.

   _____ b. He wants to buy a postcard.

5. _____ a. He can't take a picture right now.

   _____ b. He has a cheap digital camera.

6. _____ a. He wants to mail her a postcard.

   _____ b. He wants to e-mail her a photo.

7. _____ a. I can use a computer.

   _____ b. I can call my mother.

8. _____ a. Owen wants to look for a store.

   _____ b. Owen wants to go sightseeing.

Pronunciation and Writing

Say the words from the story. Write the number of syllables in each word. Underline the stressed syllable.

1. landmark _____

2. California _____

3. famous _____

4. tower _____

5. photo _____

6. sightseeing _____

7. digital _____

8. camera _____

9. computer _____

10. Internet _____

11. excited _____

12. postcard _____

13. business _____

14. hotel _____

15. picture _____

What about you?

Circle *Yes* or *No*. Then write questions and ask your partner.

Yes   No   1.   I sometimes go on a business trip.

<u>Do you sometimes go on a business trip?</u>

Yes   No   2.   I like to spend time sightseeing.

_____

Yes   No   3.   I have a digital camera.

_____

Yes   No   4.   I have an e-mail address.

_____

Yes   No   5.   I have a computer.

_____

Topics for Discussion or Writing

1.   What are some famous landmarks in your native country? What are some famous landmarks in the U.S.?

2.   Do you sometimes take pictures? If so, what do you take pictures of?

3.   Is there an Internet café in your community? If so, where is it? What are other places you can use a computer?

Lesson 12

An Exhausted Student

Belen is 34 years old. She is a student at the state university. Most students get their bachelor's degree in four or five years, but this is Belen's seventh year. Belen has a full-time job. She takes classes only at night. In one more year, Belen plans to graduate and get her degree.

Belen's life isn't easy. She is always running between school and her job. She does homework after class and on weekends. She never has time to see her friends. She always feels exhausted. But Belen knows that education is important. And with a bachelor's degree, Belen can get a major promotion at work.

Belen sees many younger students in her classes. Their families often support them. They don't have the financial commitments that she has. Belen sometimes feels a little jealous of them.

On Wednesday night, Belen walks into her biology class. The professor reminds the students about the big project due next Monday. Belen remembers. She knows she'll spend all weekend working on it.

A classmate turns to Belen and says, "This project is stressing me out!"

"I know what you mean," says Belen.

"There's a football game on Friday, a party on Saturday, and a concert on Sunday," she says. "How will I ever find the time to do the project?"

Answer the questions.

1. How old is Belen? Where is she a student?

2. In how many years do most students get their bachelor's degree?

3. Which year is this for Belen? When can she take classes?

4. When does she plan to graduate and get her degree?

5. Where is Belen always running? When does she do homework?

6. Who does she never have time to see? How does she always feel?

7. What can Belen get with a bachelor's degree?

8. What don't the younger students have that Belen has?

9. How does Belen sometimes feel about the younger students?

10. When is a big project due in her biology class?

Complete the sentences.

promotion	homework	education	bachelor's degree
school	university	night	commitments

1. Belen is 34 years old. She is a student at the state _____.

2. Most students get their _____ in four or five years.

3. Belen has a full-time job. She takes classes only at _____.

4. Belen's life isn't easy. She is always running between _____ and her job.

5. She does _____ after class and on weekends.

6. But Belen knows that _____ is important.

7. And with a bachelor's degree, Belen can get a major _____ at work.

8. The younger students don't have the financial _____ that she has.

Matching: Definitions

_____ 1. jealous

_____ 2. full-time

_____ 3. major

_____ 4. exhausted

_____ 5. financial

a. about money

b. working at least 35 hours a week

c. wanting something that someone else has

d. large or very important

e. very tired

Talking with a Classmate

Practice the dialog with a partner.

A. This project is stressing me out!

B. I know what you mean.

A. There's a football game on Friday, a party on Saturday, and a concert on Sunday.

B. Wow. You're busy.

A. Yes, I am. How will I ever find the time to do the project?

B. I don't know. But I need to spend all weekend working on it.

Checklist

Belen has a lot of financial commitments. Here are some things she pays for every month. Check (✔) the financial commitments that you have. Write other financial commitments people have on the lines below.

_____ rent	_____ transportation	_____ tuition
_____ food	_____ telephone	_____ student loan
_____ gas and electricity	_____ cell phone	_____ clothes
_____ water	_____ income taxes	_____ cable
_____ credit card	_____ health insurance	_____ family support
_____	_____	_____

Listening

Listen. Check (✔) the correct sentence.

1. _____ a. She is an older student.
   _____ b. She is a younger student.

2. _____ a. Belen needs less time.
   _____ b. Belen needs more time.

3. _____ a. She works at least 35 hours
           a week.
   _____ b. She can be a full-time
           student.

4. _____ a. She goes to a lot of parties.
   _____ b. She never has time to see
           friends.

5. _____ a. She is always very tired.
   _____ b. She is always stressed out.

6. _____ a. She can get a higher
           position.
   _____ b. She can go to football games.

7. _____ a. They have financial
           commitments.
   _____ b. Their families often support
           them.

8. _____ a. She doesn't want to study
           biology.
   _____ b. She wants the things they
           have.

Pronunciation and Writing

Say the words from the story. Write the number of syllables in each word. Underline the stressed syllable.

1. education _____
2. jealous _____
3. graduate _____
4. degree _____
5. biology _____

6. promotion _____
7. professor _____
8. exhausted _____
9. support _____
10. weekends _____

11. stressing _____
12. bachelor's _____
13. financial _____
14. university _____
15. commitments _____

What about you?

Circle *Yes* or *No.* Then write questions and ask your partner.

Yes   No   1. I have a bachelor's degree.

Do you have a bachelor's degree?

Yes   No   2. I want to graduate and get my degree.

_____

Yes   No   3. I have a full-time job.

_____

Yes   No   4. I do homework after class and on weekends.

_____

Yes   No   5. I have time to see my friends.

_____

Topics for Discussion or Writing

1. Do you think education is important? Why or why not?
2. How can a degree from a college or university help someone?
3. Is there something that is stressing you out? If so, what is it?

Lesson 13

A Visit to the Metropolitan Museum

Therese lives in an apartment in New York City. She is an excellent housekeeper and uses natural ingredients to keep her home clean. "Look," says Therese to her daughter, Sabine. "I got out all the stains in the carpet with baking soda." Then she leads Sabine into the kitchen. "I cleaned the kitchen counters with lemon juice. I cleaned the microwave with vinegar. And I cleaned the stove top with a little salt. Everything looks almost new!"

Sabine smiles and nods her head. "It's beautiful, Mom," she says. "But it's Saturday. And we live in New York City. There are many things to see and do." So Sabine and Therese decide to go to the Metropolitan Museum of Art.

Therese and Sabine take a bus to the museum. They look at the Egyptian galleries. The collection is fantastic. There are thousands of interesting items: sculpture, jewelry, statues, paintings, pictures, and other things.

Then Therese and Sabine walk into a very large room. They see the Temple of Dendur. This temple was built during the Roman period, in around 15 BC. "Isn't this incredible?" says Sabine. "Can you believe we're standing in front of an ancient temple?"

"Yes, it's very old," says Therese. "But with a little hydrogen peroxide, it could look almost new."

Answer the questions.

1. Where does Therese live?

2. What does she use to keep her home clean?

3. What did she use to get out all the stains in the carpet?

4. What did she clean the kitchen counters with?

5. What did she clean with vinegar? What did she clean with a little salt?

6. On Saturday, where do Therese and Sabine decide to go?

7. What do they look at?

8. What is in the collection?

9. What do they see in a very large room? When was it built?

10. How could the temple look with a little hydrogen peroxide?

Complete the sentences.

galleries	collection	hydrogen peroxide
museum	Temple	Roman period

1. Therese and Sabine take a bus to the _____.

2. Today they look at the Egyptian _____.

3. The _____ is fantastic.

4. They see the _____ of Dendur.

5. This temple was built during the _____, in around 15 BC.

6. Therese says with a little _____, it could look almost new.

What is the category?

sculpture	lemon juice	carpet	paintings
counters	jewelry	vinegar	stove top
baking soda	microwave	statues	salt

Things at Home to Clean	Natural Ingredients	Items in the Galleries
1. _____	1. _____	1. _____
2. _____	2. _____	2. _____
3. _____	3. _____	3. _____
4. _____	4. _____	4. _____

Talking in the Kitchen

Practice the dialog with a partner.

A. I cleaned the kitchen counters with lemon juice.

B. Wow. They look almost new.

A. I cleaned the microwave with vinegar.

B. Really? It looks great.

A. And I cleaned the stove top with a little salt.

B. It looks beautiful, Mom. But it's Saturday. Let's do something.

Checklist

Here is a list of natural ingredients some people use to keep their homes clean. Check (✔) the ingredients you have. Write other natural cleaners on the lines below.

_____ baking soda	_____ vegetable oil	_____ tea tree oil
_____ lemon juice	_____ chalk	_____ isopropyl alcohol
_____ vinegar	_____ toothpaste	_____ mineral oil
_____ salt	_____ pure soap	_____ borax
_____ hydrogen peroxide	_____ cornstarch	_____ grapefruit seed extract

_____   _____   _____

Listening

Listen. Check (✔) the correct sentence.

1. _____ a. She uses strong chemicals.
   _____ b. She uses natural ingredients.

2. _____ a. She used baking soda.
   _____ b. She used hydrogen peroxide.

3. _____ a. She used vinegar.
   _____ b. She used lemon juice.

4. _____ a. She used salt.
   _____ b. She used soap.

5. _____ a. There are many things to do.
   _____ b. We need to clean the apartment.

6. _____ a. The collection looks almost new.
   _____ b. The collection is fantastic.

7. _____ a. It's a large room.
   _____ b. It's an ancient temple.

8. _____ a. It was built in around 15 BC.
   _____ b. It was built 15 years ago.

Pronunciation and Writing

Say the words from the story. Write the number of syllables in each word. Underline the stressed syllable.

1. galleries _____
2. statues _____
3. microwave _____
4. collection _____
5. museum _____
6. vinegar _____
7. Egyptian _____
8. housekeeper _____
9. natural _____
10. temple _____
11. ingredients _____
12. Metropolitan _____
13. fantastic _____
14. ancient _____
15. sculpture _____

What about you?

Circle *Yes* or *No*. Then write questions and ask your partner.

Yes No   1. I use natural ingredients to keep my home clean.

Do you use natural ingredients to keep your home clean?

Yes No   2. I get stains out of my carpet with baking soda.

_____

Yes No   3. I clean my counters with lemon juice.

_____

Yes No   4. I think there are many things to do and see in my city.

_____

Yes No   5. I sometimes go to museums.

_____

Topics for Discussion or Writing

1. What things do you use to keep your home clean? Where do you use those things?
2. What do you like to do and see in your community?
3. Do you have museums in your community? If so, what can you look at there?

Lesson 14

Getting Directions

Myron has a terrible sense of direction. So, unfortunately, he gets lost a lot. But the bigger problem is that Myron hates asking for directions. For Myron, asking for directions is very embarrassing.

Tonight Myron has an invitation to his friend Derek's apartment for a party. Myron gets this invitation on his voicemail. In the message, Derek says, "I'm serious, Myron. Don't leave until you call me for directions."

"No, no," thinks Myron. "I can find it." But just to be sure, Myron goes online and finds a web site that gives directions. Myron types in his starting location: street address, city, state, and zip code. Then he types in the same information for his ending location, Derek's apartment. Myron clicks "Get Directions" and prints out everything he needs.

Now Myron has very clear directions. They tell him what roads to take. They tell him exactly where and which way to turn. They tell him the distances between points. And they tell him how much time it takes.

Right on time, Myron arrives at Derek's apartment. Myron knocks on the door, but there is no answer. Then Myron calls Derek on his cell phone.

"Where are you?" asks Derek.

"I'm at your apartment," answers Myron. "Where are *you*?"

"Why didn't you call me for directions?" asks Derek. "I moved last week!"

Answer the questions.

1. What does Myron have a terrible sense of? What happens a lot?

2. What does Myron hate asking for?

3. What does Myron have an invitation to tonight?

4. Where does he get this invitation? What does Derek say?

5. Where does Myron go to find a web site that gives directions?

6. What does Myron type in?

7. What does he click? What does he print out?

8. What do the very clear directions tell Myron?

9. When does Myron arrive at Derek's apartment?

10. Why isn't Derek there?

Complete the sentences.

directions	ending location	voicemail
starting location	web site	sense of direction

1. Myron has a terrible _____.

2. But the bigger problem is that Myron hates asking for _____.

3. Myron gets an invitation on his _____.

4. Myron goes online and finds a _____ that gives directions.

5. Myron types in his _____: street address, city, state, and zip code.

6. Then he types in the same information for his _____.

What is the category?

street address	turns	state	click "Get Directions"
roads	city	distance	zip code
go online	find a web site	time	print out directions

What Directions Give	Computer Activities	Information to Type In
1. _____	1. _____	1. _____
2. _____	2. _____	2. _____
3. _____	3. _____	3. _____
4. _____	4. _____	4. _____

Talking on a Cell Phone

Practice the dialog with a partner.

A. Hi. It's Myron. I'm here.

B. Where are you?

A. I'm at your apartment. Where are *you?*

B. Why didn't you call me for directions?

A. I didn't need to call you. I got great directions online.

B. But Myron, I moved last week!

Check the good ideas.

You have a terrible sense of direction and get lost a lot. Check (✔) the things that are good to do. Write other ideas on the lines below.

_____ ask for directions

_____ use a map

_____ get upset

_____ use a compass

_____ don't go anywhere

_____ get directions online

_____ call a friend for directions

_____ use a navigation system

_____ look for a place until you find it

_____ ask other people to take you places

_____   _____

Listening

Listen. Check (✔) the correct sentence.

1. _____ a. He gets lost a lot.
   _____ b. He asks for directions a lot.

2. _____ a. It's very unfortunate.
   _____ b. It's very embarrassing.

3. _____ a. It's on a web site.
   _____ b. It's on his voicemail.

4. _____ a. He goes on the Internet.
   _____ b. He gets out a map.

5. _____ a. Myron types in where he lives.
   _____ b. Myron types in where Derek lives.

6. _____ a. They tell him what time it is.
   _____ b. They tell him what roads to take.

7. _____ a. He isn't late at all.
   _____ b. He got lost again.

8. _____ a. Derek opens the door.
   _____ b. No one is there.

Pronunciation and Writing

Say the words from the story. Write the number of syllables in each word. Underline the stressed syllable.

1. directions _____
2. exactly _____
3. starting _____
4. invitation _____
5. arrives _____

6. voicemail _____
7. embarrassing _____
8. distance _____
9. terrible _____
10. ending _____

11. serious _____
12. location _____
13. unfortunately _____
14. bigger _____
15. information _____

What about you?

Circle *Yes* or *No*. Then write questions and ask your partner.

Yes No 1. I have a terrible sense of direction.

<u>Do you have a terrible sense of direction?</u>

Yes No 2. I get lost a lot.

_____

Yes No 3. I hate asking for directions.

_____

Yes No 4. I sometimes need to ask for directions.

_____

Yes No 5. I sometimes go online.

_____

Topics for Discussion or Writing

1. Do you know a web site that gives very clear directions? If so, what is it?
2. Why do some people think it's embarrassing to ask for directions?
3. For what reasons do people go online?

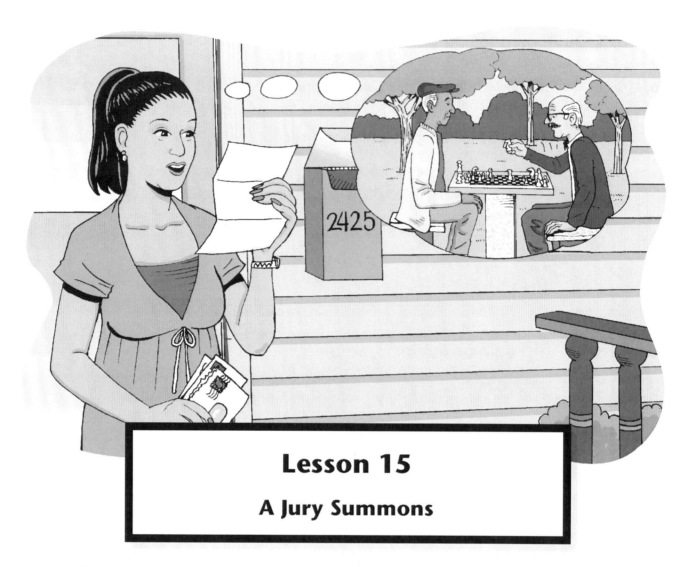

Lesson 15

A Jury Summons

Amalia lives with her father, Octavio. Octavio is 72 years old and in very good health. Right now, he is in the park playing chess with his friend Guillermo. Amalia walks outside to their mailbox. She can't believe her eyes. Octavio has a jury summons.

It's true that Octavio is qualified to serve on a jury. He is a U.S. citizen. He speaks, reads, and understands basic English. And he has never been convicted of a felony. Still, Amalia doesn't think this is a good idea at all. Octavio is retired now and deserves to relax.

Amalia is sure that Octavio can avoid jury duty somehow. She thinks for a moment. Octavio's English isn't perfect. Maybe that's a way out. Or maybe he can get a medical excuse from his doctor. Then Amalia remembers the rule about age. Octavio is over 70 years old. He simply needs to prove his age. Then he doesn't have to serve at all. Amalia is very relieved.

At 4:00, Octavio comes home. He looks through the pile of mail on the table. "Look at this," he says. "I have jury duty!"

"Don't worry, Dad," says Amalia. "You can get out of it."

"Chess with Guillermo can wait," says Octavio. "I want to perform my civic duty. I'm going!"

Answer the questions.

1. Who does Amalia live with?

2. How old is Octavio? How is his health?

3. What is he playing with his friend Guillermo?

4. What does Octavio have in the mail?

5. How is Octavio qualified to serve on a jury?

6. Why doesn't Amalia think this is a good idea at all?

7. How does Amalia think Octavio can avoid jury duty?

8. What is the rule about age that Amalia remembers?

9. What does Octavio look through when he comes home at 4:00?

10. What does Octavio want to perform?

Complete the sentences.

deserves	can avoid	understands	remembers
prove	serve	perform	convicted

1. It's true that Octavio is qualified to _____ on a jury.

2. He is a U.S. citizen. He speaks, reads, and _____ basic English.

3. And he has never been _____ of a felony.

4. But Octavio is retired now and _____ to relax.

5. Amalia is sure that Octavio _____ jury duty somehow.

6. Then Amalia _____ the rule about age.

7. Octavio is over 70 years old. He simply needs to _____ his age.

8. Octavio says, "I want to _____ my civic duty. I'm going!"

Matching: Definitions

_____ 1. citizen   a. an order to appear in a court of law

_____ 2. excuse   b. the general condition of your body or mind

_____ 3. health   c. a very serious crime

_____ 4. summons   d. an explanation for not doing something

_____ 5. chess   e. a legal member of a country

_____ 6. felony   f. a game for two players on a board with 64 squares

Talking About a Jury Summons

Practice the dialog with a partner.

A. **Look at this. I have jury duty!**

B. Don't worry, Dad. You can get out of it.

A. **What do you mean?**

B. You're over 70 years old. You don't have to serve at all.

A. **Well, am I qualified to serve on a jury?**

B. Of course you are.

A. **Then I want to perform my civic duty. I'm going!**

Check the good excuses.

Sometimes you can't serve on a jury. Check (✔) the good excuses you can have for not serving. Write other ideas on the lines below.

_____ have a serious medical problem   _____ are retired and deserve to relax

_____ play chess a lot   _____ are over 70 but in good health

_____ are not a U.S. citizen   _____ have been convicted of a felony

_____ have a full-time job   _____ have childcare problems

_____ don't speak or understand basic English   _____ speak English very well but not perfectly

_____   _____

Listening

Listen. Check (✔) the correct sentence.

1. ____ a. Octavio is playing chess.
   ____ b. Octavio has a jury summons.

2. ____ a. He is a U.S. citizen.
   ____ b. He has been convicted of a felony.

3. ____ a. She thinks he deserves to relax.
   ____ b. She thinks he can serve later.

4. ____ a. Octavio's English is fluent.
   ____ b. Octavio's English isn't perfect.

5. ____ a. His doctor can give him a way out.
   ____ b. He can go to the hospital.

6. ____ a. He can't serve at all.
   ____ b. He doesn't have to serve at all.

7. ____ a. He says, "I have jury duty!"
   ____ b. He says, "I can get out of it!"

8. ____ a. He wants to play chess in the park.
   ____ b. He wants to serve on a jury.

Pronunciation and Writing

Say the words from the story. Write the number of syllables in each word. Underline the stressed syllable.

1. qualified ____
2. summons ____
3. excuse ____
4. mailbox ____
5. relieved ____

6. deserves ____
7. perform ____
8. retired ____
9. civic ____
10. felony ____

11. convicted ____
12. medical ____
13. jury ____
14. avoid ____
15. citizen ____

What about you?

Circle *Yes* or *No.* Then write questions and ask your partner.

Yes No 1. I sometimes play chess.

<u>Do you sometimes play chess?</u>

Yes No 2. I think I'm qualified to serve on a jury.

_____

Yes No 3. I speak, read, and understand basic English.

_____

Yes No 4. I sometimes have a jury summons.

_____

Yes No 5. I want to serve on a jury.

_____

Topics for Discussion or Writing

1. For what reasons do some people want to avoid jury duty?
2. What kinds of crimes are felonies?
3. What kinds of civic duties can people perform?

Listening Exercise Prompts

Lesson 1, page 8

Listen. Check the correct sentence.

1. Samir and Conrad never see each other.
2. "I'm about six feet tall," says Conrad.
3. "I'm pretty muscular."
4. "And I have a mustache."
5. He is about five feet seven inches tall.
6. He is mostly bald.
7. He doesn't have a mustache.
8. "You're a little different from your description," says Samir.

Lesson 2, page 14

Listen. Check the correct sentence.

1. Jennifer and Shaun are newlyweds.
2. They are exhausted when they get home.
3. Their apartment is a mess.
4. They eat peanut-butter sandwiches for dinner.
5. Jennifer says, "But it's not a good time. Look at this place!"
6. Evelyn lives three thousand miles away.
7. When Jennifer and Shaun are at work, Evelyn cleans the apartment.
8. Now Jennifer thinks Evelyn is the best mother-in-law in the world.

Lesson 3, page 20

Listen. Check the correct sentence.

1. Jonas still needs to fly home to Atlanta.
2. His flight, 631, is delayed by an hour.
3. Jonas is disappointed.
4. At the gate, Jonas hears an announcement.
5. He reads a few pages, but his eyes feel very heavy.
6. Suddenly, Jonas wakes up and looks around.
7. Jonas missed his flight!
8. An airline worker tells Jonas he needs to buy a new ticket to Atlanta.

Lesson 4, page 26

Listen. Check the correct sentence.

1. Every summer, Abby goes home to visit her family.
2. Her family has a garden. Her father catches fish in the lake.
3. Abby thinks the food in the city is terrible.
4. There are Becker's Supermarkets all over her city.
5. At Becker's, there are too many processed foods.
6. Their foods have too many artificial ingredients.
7. But Abby needs to eat, so she usually shops at Becker's.
8. Abby says, "You can't eat like this in the city, Mom."

Lesson 5, page 32

Listen. Check the correct sentence.

1. Fortunately, Dolores is in very good condition for her age.
2. Mireya thinks her grandmother's comment is very strange.
3. Some elderly people have dementia.
4. Mireya takes Dolores to the doctor.
5. Dolores has an MRI.
6. The doctor gives her an evaluation.
7. Soon, Mireya learns that the test results are good.
8. The neighbor says, "I'm taking a dance class. And since it's so hot in the house, I like to practice on the roof."

Lesson 6, page 38

Listen. Check the correct sentence.

1. Graciela cleans three floors of a large office building.
2. Last year, she received an excellent performance evaluation and two pay raises.
3. Now, Graciela and Rogelio are working together.
4. Unfortunately, Rogelio isn't a very good worker.
5. He takes too many breaks.

6. Rogelio asks, "Do you think it's time to ask for a pay raise?"

7. Graciela says, "You need to work for at least three months before you are eligible for a pay raise."

8. Graciela says, "At this point, you really don't deserve one."

Lesson 7, page 44
Listen. Check the correct sentence.

1. The salesclerk brings in a matching jacket. She also has a pretty pink blouse.

2. The salesclerk is very persuasive.

3. "Why not?" she says. "I'll take it all!"

4. At home, Shirin looks in her bag and sighs.

5. After all, Shirin is a nurse in a big hospital.

6. The next day, Shirin returns the jacket and blouse to Drake's.

7. "No, thank you," says Shirin firmly. "Just a refund, please."

8. When Shirin gets home that evening, there is a message on her answering machine.

Lesson 8, page 50
Listen. Check the correct sentence.

1. Loretta pays her bills on time and rarely spends money on things for herself.

2. Loretta is also very generous.

3. Right now, Loretta is very worried about her nephew, Charlie.

4. Unfortunately, Charlie doesn't qualify for a bank loan.

5. "I think the transplant costs about $10,000," says Charlie.

6. "Is it his heart? Is it his liver or a kidney?"

7. Loretta gets out her checkbook.

8. "Every month, you'll get a payment with interest," says Charlie.

Lesson 9, page 56
Listen. Check the correct sentence.

1. Midori sees Kano's old brown jacket.

2. Besides, Midori bought him a new gray jacket last year.

3. She drops off the bag at the thrift store.

4. The thrift store resells clothing and other usable items.

5. Then they use the money for charity.

6. Midori always feels good about donating things she doesn't need.

7. "Hmm," Kano says. "I can't find my brown jacket."

8. "I went to the thrift store and bought my old brown jacket. Then I donated my gray one."

Lesson 10, page 62
Listen. Check the correct sentence.

1. Magda's apartment building has termites.

2. Magda's landlord decides to fumigate the entire apartment complex.

3. The fumigation is a little inconvenient.

4. She needs to remove her plants.

5. She needs to move out of her apartment and stay at a hotel for two days.

6. Magda's landlord gives Magda and the other tenants an allowance, so they don't have to pay for their hotel rooms.

7. On Tuesday, Magda checks into the Vacation Inn.

8. "Don't go outside," says Mr. Foster. "There are mosquitoes everywhere!"

Lesson 11, page 68
Listen. Check the correct sentence.

1. Philip and his co-worker Owen are on a four-day business trip to Paris, France.

2. On their last day, Philip and Owen decide they can spend a few hours sightseeing.

3. Philip and Owen take a taxi to the Eiffel Tower.

4. "I want to take a picture of this," says Philip.

5. Unfortunately, Philip doesn't have a camera.

6. Philip says, "Then I can go back to the hotel and call my mother for her e-mail address."

7. "Then I can go to an Internet café."

8. "Or," says Owen, "you can buy your mother a postcard. Then you can put on a stamp and mail it to her. And then we can see more of Paris."

Lesson 12, page 74

Listen. Check the correct sentence.

1. Belen is thirty-four years old.
2. Most students get their bachelor's degree in four or five years, but this is Belen's seventh year.
3. Belen has a full-time job.
4. She does homework after class and on weekends.
5. She always feels exhausted.
6. With a bachelor's degree, Belen can get a major promotion at work.
7. Belen sees many younger students in her classes.
8. Belen sometimes feels a little jealous of them.

Lesson 13, page 80

Listen. Check the correct sentence.

1. Therese is an excellent housekeeper.
2. Therese says, "I got out all the stains in the carpet."
3. She says, "I cleaned the kitchen counters."
4. She says, "And I cleaned the stove top."
5. Sabine says, "But it's Saturday. And we live in New York City."
6. They look at the Egyptian galleries.
7. They see the Temple of Dendur.
8. This temple was built during the Roman period.

Lesson 14, page 86

Listen. Check the correct sentence.

1. Myron has a terrible sense of direction.
2. But the bigger problem is that Myron hates asking for directions.
3. Tonight Myron has an invitation to his friend Derek's apartment for a party.
4. Just to be sure, Myron goes online and finds a web site that gives directions.
5. Myron types in his starting location: street address, city, state, and zip code.
6. Now Myron has very clear directions.
7. Right on time, Myron arrives at Derek's apartment.
8. Myron knocks on the door, but there is no answer.

Lesson 15, page 92

Listen. Check the correct sentence.

1. Amalia walks outside to their mailbox. She can't believe her eyes.
2. It's true that Octavio is qualified to serve on a jury.
3. Still, Amalia doesn't think this is a good idea at all.
4. Amalia is sure that Octavio can avoid jury duty somehow.
5. Maybe he can get a medical excuse from his doctor.
6. Then Amalia remembers the rule about age.
7. Octavio looks through the pile of mail on the table.
8. He wants to perform his civic duty.